Between

us

Ordinary Peeps

Daily Devotionals
By
Lisa Wirtner

AUTUMN ARCH PUBLISHING
Iowa
www.AutumnArchPublishing.com

A product of AUTUMN ARCH PUBLISHING
Cover design: Aaron Bunce
Interior design & editing: Aaron Bunce

TRADE PAPERBACK ISBN: 978-0-9992026-1-6
E-Book ISBN: B074LWM6QL

1st Edition - 2017

THIS BOOK was inspired by God, working in and through me each and every day. The entire journey was supported with the loving encouragement of my Husband, Family, and Friends. Its completion is being brought to you by, Aaron Bunce, a local author and publisher that believed in the positive message of my writing and took a chance on me.

Thank you and God bless you all!

A note from the author

In this busy world it is necessary to connect with others, so that we know we are not alone, we make a difference, and that we matter even if we are ordinary ☺

I hope this book is encouraging, reaches you where you are, and will even challenge you a bit to grow deeper in your faith journey - to know the ordinary can be used for great things. It will include thoughts, prayers, and scriptures. Just between us!

1

OFTEN IN OUR BUSYNESS, we just try to get by. We look at others and think, "How are they handling it so well?" and worse yet, we think, "I wish my life was as good as theirs".

Comparing our lives to others' lives is really toxic in many ways.

First, we must realize it is only perception, and it may not be reality. They are likely having the same thoughts and struggles.

Second, we have to realize there is really so much to be thankful for in our lives. We just have to slow down enough to think of the positives. Doing this can change our lives for the better!

Third, and the most important, concentrating on and comparing ourselves to others will keep us from realizing our own self-worth. The scriptures say we are fearfully and wonderfully made for a purpose.

Heavenly Father,

Please open our eyes to see our purpose that you have chosen us for. Help us to concentrate on the positives in our "now" and to continue to look to you Lord for direction. Help us to see others fairly and not judge them. For we do not know all of the struggles they face.

It is encouraging to the ordinary that you do not think of us like that, Lord. Continue to use us to

share truths of your Word that both inspire and
challenge us for good.

In Jesus Name,

Amen!

Psalm 139:14

"I praise you because I am fearfully and wonderfully made;
your works are wonderful, I know that full well."

NO MATTER YOUR ROLE, status, or job, whether it is inside or outside the home, in your own business, or for a corporation, we must remember who we are really working for. Our ultimate Boss is Jesus Christ, our Lord.

Heavenly Father,

Bless this week and help us remember that what we do really does matters to you. Help us to work, act, and speak with the upmost integrity and positivity.

In Jesus Name,

Amen

Colossians 3:23

"Whatever you do, work at it with all your heart, as working for the Lord, not for human masters."

3

OFTEN CIRCUMSTANCES, events, and even people in our lives, can rob us of Joy, Peace, and Hope. We have to look beyond, and Trust God for our fulfillment. Only He can fill us with everything we need, and provide the peace that passes all understanding in all circumstances.

Heavenly Father,

Our day-to-day lives are filled with demands and stresses that leave us feeling defeated, empty and dry. I pray that we continue to come to you and your Word to replenish and be filled. Help us to trust you, believe you, and turn to you first.

In Jesus Name,

Amen

Romans 15:13

"I pray that God, the source of hope, will fill you completely with joy and peace because you trust in him. Then you will overflow with confident hope through the power of the Holy Spirit."

4

MOST OF US STRUGGLE with self-doubt. The feeling that we are just not good enough, smart enough, or even not pretty enough. These thoughts come from Satan, who uses lies to keep us from the Joy we deserve. Sometimes, these feelings are inspired by shame or guilt from our sins. Sometimes, they come from others trying to build themselves up. However, we do have hope and freedom, if we seek God when those thoughts come upon us. He will hear us, answer us, and deliver us from the fears.

Heavenly Father,

Thank you for the freedom from our fears when we seek you. It is because of you that we are beautiful. Help us as these thoughts creep back in that we continue to seek you first.

In Jesus Name,

Amen

Psalm 34:4-5

"I sought the Lord, and he answered me; He delivered me from all my fears. Those that look to him are radiant; their faces are never covered with shame."

5

BELOW is the chorus to a popular new song, *Trust In You!* (written by Lauren Daigle, Michael Farren, & Paul Mabury).

> *When you don't move the mountains I'm needing you to move*
>
> *When you don't part the waters I wish I could walk through*
>
> *When you don't give the answers as I cry out to you*
>
> *I will trust, I will trust, I will trust in You*

Reflecting on all of the times that things didn't change, we did not get the "yes" we hoped for, or had to wait for answers .... But God held steady, keeping us unshaken, without fear because He is in Control. Trust In Him.

Heavenly Father,

It is so reassuring, Lord, that you are in control and will hold those who trust and believe in you in complete peace, unshaken and hopeful.

In Jesus Name,

Amen

Psalm 112:6-7

Surely the righteous will never be shaken; they will be
remembered forever. They will have no fear of bad news; their
hearts are steadfast, trusting in the Lord.

6

THERE ARE TIMES we need to make a move, a change, or take action. However, if we are uncertain and don't feel confident in the direction or plan, then we need to remain still. This can be very hard, but we must know these are the times God is working on things for us. He is preparing the plan, paving the road, and working out the details if only we wait patiently, because His plan is far greater than we could ever imagine.

Heavenly Father,

Help us, Lord, to be still and trust in you and to wait on your perfect timing. We often try to get ahead of you, Lord. Forgive us when we do this. Please provide peace in the stillness and contentment in the wait.

In Jesus Name,

Amen

Psalm 46:10

Be still, and know that I am God! I will be honored by every nation. I will be honored throughout the world.

7

DISAPPOINTMENT... it comes in so many forms. It may be bad news, unpleasant attitudes, or no response at all. But why be discouraged? Our hope should only be in Jesus, our Savior, our God, not in man.

Heavenly Father,

Calm us, Lord. Shield us from man's disappointments. Rather, help us look to you! You are the provider of Hope, the prince of Peace, and the one and only source of Joy. We love you, Lord.

In Jesus Name,

Amen

Psalm 43:5

Why am I discouraged? Why is my heart so sad? I will put my hope in God! I will praise him again my Savior and my God!

8

WE CHOOSE our strongholds. Yes, we have a choice. Unfortunately, at times we choose to continue to make the wrong choices, depending on and sometimes turning to the wrong things to comfort and complete us.

"Why?" "What are we afraid of?" "Why are we afraid to be without the comfort these strongholds provide?" Trust God. Surrender. Depend on Him. Ask Him to free you from the strongholds!

> Heavenly Father,
>
> Why, Lord, are we so foolish? I pray, Lord, we look at what we focus and depend on. When it is a source we go to before you may we examine our motives, surrender, and ask you to help free us. Thank you for the freedom and assurance that with you we shall not fear!
>
> In Jesus Name,
>
> Amen
>
> Psalm 27:1

The LORD is my light and my salvation—so why should I be afraid? The LORD is my fortress, protecting me from danger, so why should I tremble?

9

EXHAUSTION AND WEAR can affect each of us differently. Some may be physically tired from repetitive walking, standing, or lifting. Some may be mentally tired from continual decisions and thinking. Others could be worn out from worry, sickness, from trying so hard, or giving too much. Whatever the effect is for you, remember there is rest for our souls in Jesus, if only we come to him.

Heavenly Father,

We seek you today to give us rest to our souls, our spirit and even our tired and worn physical bodies. Life has so many demands that simply wear us out. Fill us back up with your life sustaining truth. Lord, let us rest in you!

In Jesus Name,

Amen

Matthew 11:28

Come to me, all you who are weary and burdened, and I will give you rest.

10

FEAR GOD.... at first when we hear this statement, we may think: "to be afraid of God". It may make us think how unworthy we are. Thanks to a study this past summer, we've learned to look at Fearing God in a different way. To Fear God is to Honor Him, to Love Him, to show Reverence to Him.

Heavenly Father,

Thank you, Lord, for the fresh perspective you bring to the meaning of fearing you. To know that we don't have to be afraid of you, and that we can take solace knowing that you already took care of your believer's sins. This allows us to freely honor, praise, and deeply respect you! We Love You, Lord! You alone are awesome and worthy of all praise!

In Jesus Name,

Amen

1 Chronicles 16:25

Great is the LORD! He is most worthy of praise! He is to be feared above all gods.

11

FAITH IS NO MATTER WHAT, believing and trusting, and remaining strong. Seeing or not seeing. Regardless, knowing God is with us, guiding and protecting us always.

> Heavenly Father,
>
> Thank you, Lord, for keeping us protected in the fire. For keeping us pure as gold. It is through Faith we hold up. Through Faith, we remain strong. Through Faith, you are glorified and Jesus is shown.
>
> In Jesus Name,
>
> Amen

1 Peter 1:7

These trials will show that your faith is genuine. It is being tested as fire tests and purifies gold though your faith is far more precious than mere gold. So when your faith remains strong through many trials, it will bring you much praise and glory and honor on the day when Jesus Christ is revealed to the whole world.

12

WHEN WE FEEL OVERWHELMED, confused, unsure, and consider giving up, we need to earnestly cry out to our Lord Jesus in prayer. Seek His understanding, directions, and purpose in the struggles that we face in our daily lives. He is always near and longs for us to seek Him.

Heavenly Father,

We so often cannot see through the fog of our daily demands and struggles. But you, Lord, are the light. You see the path. You have the plan. You give us a future and a hope because we believe in you. You know our pains and uncertainties, but want us to call upon you in prayer. When we do, you listen and deliver us. Thank you, Lord, for loving us so much.

In Jesus Name,

Amen

Jeremiah 29:11-13

For I know the plans I have for you, says the Lord. They are plans for good and not for disaster, to give you a future and a hope. In those days when you pray, I will listen. If you look for me wholeheartedly, you will find me.

13

SOMETIMES IN LIFE it is easy to fear the future. It may because of a health diagnosis, a financial situation, a job uncertainty, violence in the news, or simply choices made by the government. But God tells us we do not have to be afraid. He is with us. He is our help in times of need.

Heavenly Father,

Please hold and comfort all of us who are afraid tonight. Help us to not be discouraged, but rather to be confident in you, Lord. You are our victory! We thank you for the price you paid for freedom on the cross!

In Jesus Name,

Amen

Isaiah 41:10

Don't be afraid, for I am with you. Don't be discouraged, for I am your God. I will strengthen you and help you. I will hold you up with my victorious right hand.

14

THE SAYING GOES: "Out of the mouths of babes", we hear such innocence, truth, and pure sweetness. We as adults can learn so much from their perspective, even though at times it is hard to swallow.

Heavenly Father,

Thank you, Lord, for the children and their sweet little voices, cuddles, and innocent perspective. Help us to be like them and simply believe.

In Jesus Name,

Amen

Matthew 18:3

And he said: Truly I tell you, unless you change and become like little children, you will never enter the kingdom of heaven.

15

THERE ISN'T A DAY, a circumstance, or an event that can surprise God. Each one has gone through His hands and His care. This gives us the reassurance that He is in Control and cares about each and every moment in our day.

Heavenly Father,

Lord, help us realize that you have already seen each moment of every day. I am thankful and joyful in each day that you have made. Help us to rejoice and be glad in them in all circumstances, good and bad.

In Jesus Name,

Amen

Psalm 118:24

This is the day the Lord has made. We will rejoice and be glad in it.

16

HE HEARS OUR CRIES FOR MERCY, he intently listens to us. He draws near when we call upon His name.

Heavenly Father,

Thank you, Lord, that even in this world of so many people, you care and listen to all of our cries. Thank you for caring for us, having mercy on us, forgiving and loving us.

In Jesus Name,

Amen

Psalm 116

I love the Lord because he hears my voice and my prayer for mercy. Because he bends down to listen, I will pray as long as I have breath!

17

IT IS EASY to sway from the path. We often try to take the controls or simply let go and let the wind take us. The good news is that even with a detour, if we look to Jesus for guidance through His word, prayer and direction of the Holy Spirit, we can get right back on track.

Heavenly Father,

Please guide our hearts and minds today according to your word. Help us to hear and obey what you have for us. We know, Lord, your way is the only right and true way.

In Jesus Name,

Amen

Psalm 119:105

Your word is a lamp to guide my feet and a light for my path.

18

MUSIC... this is often the most expressive form of Worship. The ly
can be directly from the Word of God, from the hymns, or through
life changing experiences of those writing the songs.

Heavenly Father,

Thank you for the music that praises you, Lord. The
songs and melodies that speak to us right where we are,
that challenge us for change, and that encourage us in our
daily walk with you. These songs draw us closer to you,
comfort and continue to awe us. The lyrics bring joy and
peace to our souls.

In Jesus Name,

Amen

Psalm 100:2

Worship the Lord with gladness; come before him with joyful
songs.

19

NO MATTER WHAT, when we seek His presence we feel peace and joy. We can trust in his plan, hope in His direction, and find joy in His presence.

Heavenly Father,

Thank you for your plans for us. They are so much better than the ones we make for ourselves. Help us to trust and obey you to prosper and be successful. Quiet our racing thoughts so we can feel the joy in your presence. We love you, Lord.

In Jesus Name,

Amen

Psalm 16:11

You make known to me the path of life; you will fill me with joy in your presence, with eternal pleasures at your right hand.

20

BEING THANKFUL AND GRATEFUL are keys to happiness. However, praising God with all of our hearts and sharing the good news of Jesus Christ and what He has done for us, is freedom and pure worship. Happiness is temporary, but freedom in Christ is eternal.

Heavenly Father,

We praise you, Lord, and are so very grateful for all you do, have done, and continue to do. Your ways are so marvelous. Help us, Lord, to share these experiences, stories, and testimonials with others for your Glory.

In Jesus Name,

Amen

Psalm 9:1

I will praise you, Lord, with all my heart; I will tell of all the marvelous things you have done.

21

THE FRUIT OF THE SPIRIT is love, joy, peace, patience, kindness, goodness, faithfulness, gentleness, and self-control.

When we believe in and live for God, He produces and cultivates these things in us. I love how "The Message" version gives a slightly different perspective. It extenuates the fact that the fruits are gifts from God given freely when we live His way.

Heavenly Father,

Thank you and praise you, Lord, for giving us such clear guidance. These ways are not always the ways of the world. Please continue to cultivate these fruits in us. Keep using us as examples of Jesus to those around us. We thank you for loving us so much and for the sacrifice on the cross.

In Jesus Name,

Amen

Galatians 5:22-23

But what happens when we live God's way? He brings gifts into our lives, much the same way that fruit appears in an orchard—things like affection for others, exuberance about life, serenity. We develop willingness to stick with things, a sense of compassion in the heart, and a conviction that a basic holiness permeates things and people. We find ourselves involved in loyal commitments, not needing to force our way in life, able to marshal and direct our energies wisely.

22

FORGIVENESS.... we all want it from God. We want it from people, but we don't always want to give it as freely to others. We are challenged to be like Jesus, to offer grace to others like we have been given from God through Christ Jesus. Our thoughts, words, and actions towards others are to be kind, to build up and to not tear down.

Heavenly Father,

Thank you for the grace and forgiveness you give us. Help us to have that same compassion for others.

In Jesus Name,

Amen

Ephesians 4: 30-32

And do not bring sorrow to God's Holy Spirit by the way you live. Remember, he has identified you as his own, guaranteeing that you will be saved on the day of redemption. Get rid of all bitterness, rage, anger, harsh words, and slander, as well as all types of evil behavior. Instead, be kind to each other, tenderhearted, forgiving one another, just as God through Christ has forgiven you.

23

HAVE YOU EVER WISHED that you could take back words the moment they left your tongue or lips? Knowing immediately you should have remained silent, or better yet, that you should never even let the thoughts cross your mind.

Heavenly Father,

Forgive us, Lord, when we speak instead of being quiet. Help us to think first, remembering that words should build up others, and not tear them down. Our thoughts should be kind, and our words gentle.

In Jesus Name,

Amen

Psalm 141:3

Set a guard, O Lord, over my mouth; keep watch over the door of my lips!

24

WE ARE FACED WITH SITUATIONS, circumstances, and trials each day. But because of Christ, we are called to live in peace and be thankful. He paid the ultimate sacrifice for us so we can be free and have everlasting peace in Him.

Heavenly Father,

Please hold us daily in your truths, so your peace that passes all understanding will be upon us. We love you Lord. We are thankful that you are in control!

In Jesus Name,

Amen

Colossians 3:15

And let the peace that comes from Christ rule in your hearts. For as members of one body you are called to live in peace. And always be thankful.

25

WHEN THE PATH IS UNCERTAIN and the way unsure, we can Trust in Him. So often we face situations that are not easy, can be scary, and do not have easy solutions. In these times we need to seek Him, listen for His instructions, and not grow weary in waiting for His direction.

Heavenly Father,

Lord God, come into the circumstances we cannot see through. Guide us with answers, direction, and the way to go. We trust in you.

In Jesus Name,

Amen

Proverbs 3:5-6

Trust in the Lord with all your heart; do not depend on your own understanding. Seek his will in all you do, and he will show you which path to take.

26

GOALS... we often have to set them, for both professional and personal reasons. Some are short term. Some are long term. We set them, but often struggle with keeping them. Why? We lose focus on the prize, and the example. We get tangled up within ourselves and our destructive ways. But when we refocus on the eternal and the ultimate example of Jesus, we can clearly run for the prize, be free from sin, and be free indeed.

Heavenly Father,

Please keep us focused on you and the goals before us. Help us to persevere and maintain the endurance needed in the race. With you, Lord, we will always receive the prize.

In Jesus Name

Amen

Hebrews 12:1

Therefore, since we have so great a cloud of witnesses surrounding us, let us also lay aside every encumbrance and the sin which so easily entangles us, and let us run with endurance the race that is set before us.

27

EVERYWHERE YOU TURN, everyone you talk to, and in everything we do there are so many things to worry about. Will things get done? How will people react? What will be the outcome? These pressures and worries can mount. They can become a major source of anxiety. But God says, "Give them to me", "Cast them on me", "I will take them all because I care for you". Wow, these truths are so amazing! How can He care for us in the grand scheme of the universe? Well, the answer is simply, He does. Trust Him. Give your worries over to him. Enjoy the peace in His presence.

Heavenly Father,

Thank you for caring so deeply for us. Thank you for the reassurance that there isn't a worry that is too big for you. Thank you for being the one true constant in our lives. We thank you and praise you, Lord.

In Jesus Name,

Amen

1 Peter 5:7

Cast all your anxiety on him because he cares for you.

28

WE OFTEN GET IMPATIENT with others. We think they should do things differently, or think of things in our ways. However, we are given the instructions from God to be humble and gentle. We are to be patient with them, forgiving their faults and to love them no matter what. Why? Simply because that is what our Lord does for us.

Heavenly Father,

Thank you for your grace. Help us to give this to others without any expectation from them. Help us simply to love them. Help us to resemble you, Lord, in humbleness and kindness.

In Jesus Name,

Amen

Ephesians 4:2

Always be humble and gentle. Be patient with each other, making allowance for each other's faults because of your love

29

SOMETIMES OUR PRAYER LIST is too overwhelming and the words just won't come, or we simply don't have the right attitude. During these times the Holy Spirit intercedes on our behalf, knowing exactly what we need and communicates it to our Lord in a way we cannot.

Heavenly Father,

Thank you for the Holy Spirit, who lives in us and goes before us in our weakness, knowing what we need and exactly how to express it to you in your perfect timing.

In Jesus Name,

Amen

Romans 8:26

And the Holy Spirit helps us in our weakness. For example, we don't know what God wants us to pray for. But the Holy Spirit prays for us with groaning that cannot be expressed in words.

30

SEASONS OF WAITING can come at any time. During these times we feel pain and anxiety. We are left wondering why or when. We can even begin doubting our value. However, God just asks us to Trust Him, to wait, to know that He is still working, and to keep on keeping on. When we do, He will strengthen us, renew us, and keep us from becoming weary.

Heavenly Father,

Thank you for always loving us. No matter if it is a time of clarity, or a time of waiting, we trust you. It is you, Lord that provides strength for us to soar above the problems, to run the race ahead of us and to walk with you through the journey.

In Jesus Name,

Amen

Isaiah 40:31

Yet those who wait for the Lord Will gain new strength; they will mount up with wings like eagles, they will run and not get tired, they will walk and not become weary.

31

DO YOU EVER JUMP TO CONCLUSIONS, assume the worst in others, or make a judgment before knowing the entire story? Yes, we are humans. That is our nature. But aren't we glad God is not that way with us! He is so merciful, so forgiving, letting us slip back more often than we care to admit. Yet, he still loves us and is compassionate to us.

Heavenly Father,

Thank you, Lord, for your compassion, grace, mercy, and unfailing love. Help us, Lord, to learn to follow your ways and be slow to anger in our daily lives. Help us to love first and not judge. Help us to truly care and show mercy, not just go through the motions. We long to be like you, Lord.

In Jesus Name,

Amen

Psalm 103:8

The Lord is compassionate and merciful, slow to get angry and filled with unfailing love.

32

OUR DAY-TO-DAY TASKS can often seem so overwhelming, out of reach, and simply impossible to complete. Accomplishing them can often make us feel hopeless. However, when we look to God we are reminded that all things are possible. He can make the most impossible of tasks attainable. He can provide peace amidst the pressure, and produce an outcome that is better than ever.

Heavenly Father,

We trust in you for the areas in life that seem impossible. Lord, you do not see them that way. You see them as areas you can change, turn for the better, or simply resolve in ways beyond our imagination. Thank you, Lord, for making the impossible possible.

In Jesus Name,

Amen

Matthew 19:26

Jesus looked at them and said, "With man this is impossible, but with God all things are possible."

33

LIGHT AND DARKNESS... their literal meanings are easy to define. Day and night, or bright and dark, but the emotional and spiritual meanings are very different. It is harder to see, easier to hide, and can more frequently be confused with the other. However, if we look to Jesus, He provides the ultimate light for us. It reveals, but also heals and eternally provides life.

Heavenly Father,

Thank you, Lord, for providing the light that is pure and keeps us from darkness. Thank you for the eternal message of hope that is only found in you, Lord.

In Jesus Name,

Amen

John 8:12

Jesus spoke to the people once more and said, "I am the light of the world. If you follow me, you won't have to walk in darkness, because you will have the light that leads to life."

34

WHY DO WE WORRY, fret, or stew over things? So often we can't see beyond the happenstances of each day. We get so stuck in the tangled web of our daily circumstances that we feel out of control. We become anxious and overwhelmed. But, we must always remember that God is always ready to listen. He instructs us to pray and tell Him everything.

Heavenly Father,

Thank you, Lord, for the invitation to come to you with everything and to not be anxious. You know our needs, and yet want us to tell them to you. To express our feelings to you like a friend, a loved one, or a child. Thank you, Lord, for loving us so much. We praise you for all you have done.

In Jesus Name,

Amen

Philippians 4:6

Don't worry about anything; instead, pray about everything. Tell God what you need, and thank him for all he has done.

WE PRAY FOR directness and truth in our lives, but it is sometimes painful to hear and hard to take.

Do we really want to hear it?

Do we really want to change?

In James in the NIV, we are told to submit to God. In the Message we are told to "get serious". Both translations are very clear, direct, and specific. We need to draw near to God, surrender to Him, cry out to Him, ask for repentance, and change. This is the direction of freedom. Yes, surrendering brings true freedom.

Heavenly Father,

Thank you for your clear messages to us. Thank you for the grace you allow when we fail. Thank you for the true freedom you give when we follow your instructions. Give us humble hearts that want change and freedom. We love you, Lord.

In Jesus Name,

Amen

James 4:7-10

Submit yourselves, then, to God. Resist the devil, and he will flee from you. 8 Come near to God and he will come near to you. Wash your hands, you sinners, and purify your hearts, you double-minded. 9 Grieve, mourn and wail. Change your laughter to mourning and your joy to gloom. 10 Humble yourselves before the Lord, and he will lift you up.

So let God work his will in you. Yell a loud no to the Devil and watch him scamper. Say a quiet yes to God and he'll be there in no time. Quit dabbling in sin. Purify your inner life. Quit playing the field. Hit bottom, and cry your eyes out. The fun and games are over. Get serious, really serious. Get down on your knees before the Master; it's the only way you'll get on your feet.

36

ALTHOUGH SOME PEOPLE are happy and joyful most of the time, some simply are not. They struggle to put a smile on their faces because of the sadness in their hearts.

If you are happy, join me in praying for and having compassion towards those who are struggling.

Heavenly Father,

Thank you, Lord, for holding the brokenhearted and helping them heal. We know this is so because of your word. Thank you, Lord. You know exactly who we are praying for today. You know all of the needs. Help us to show the same compassion and grace. I pray that you provide the words that build up and do not tear down. Help us to have the courage to step out in faith and help them.

In Jesus Name,

Amen

Proverbs 15:13

A cheerful heart brings a smile to your face; a sad heart makes it hard to get through the day.

Psalm 147:3

He heals the brokenhearted and bandages their wounds.

37

IF ASKED "Do you believe?" Most of us would answer without hesitation, "Yes", "Absolutely", or "Of course". We believe in God, the Father, the Son, and the Holy Spirit. We believe in His power to do and be great things. But often we don't truly believe it for ourselves. We love and believe, but we don't go as far as believing that He loved us first and that He has a calling, a plan, and a purpose for each of us. We don't grasp that we are given the same mighty power He has, because we are His followers.

Heavenly Father,

Thank you, Lord, for your word. It provides the clarity we need to understand your greatness. Help us to keep our focus on you, your plans, and the unique calling you have for us. We often think greatness is for others, but you Lord have promised this for each of your followers. Thank you, Lord!

In Jesus Name,

Amen

Ephesians 1:19

But I do more than thank. I ask—ask the God of our Master, Jesus Christ, the God of glory—to make you intelligent and discerning in knowing him personally, your eyes focused and clear, so that you can see exactly what it is he is calling you to do, grasp the immensity of this glorious way of life he has for his followers, oh, the utter extravagance of his work in us who trust him—endless energy, boundless strength.

38

FEELING PAINED, confused, or simply perplexed over a season in your life? Wondering how it will work out? Don't fear. Have faith in our Savior. Hold tight to His promise that all things will work together for good for all that love Him.

Heavenly Father,

Help us to trust and hold on to your promise, Lord. Give us the glimpse of the good in even the hardest of life's circumstances. There is never a time we go through that doesn't have purpose. Thank you, Lord. We love you!

In Jesus Name,

Amen

Romans 8:28

And we know that for those who love God all things work together for good, for those who are called according to his purpose.

39

PRIDE... it is a sin. It comes in all shapes and sizes. It can be arrogance, but it can also disguise itself as low self-worth. Regardless, it cheats and robs us of contentment, genuine friendships, and ultimately God's purpose and Glory. It is complete self-absorption. We need to follow Jesus' example and be humble, not proud.

Heavenly Father,

Forgive us for allowing pride to overtake us. Help us to be humble before you, Lord. Open our eyes to this sin and everything it does to keep us from all you have for us.

In Jesus Name,

Amen

Proverbs 11:2

Pride leads to disgrace, but with humility comes wisdom.

40

LOVING AND BELIEVING in God seems natural and easy for some, but a struggle for others. One way to really get to know and love Him is to learn his names. King of Kings, Lord of Lords, Prince of Peace, Mighty Counselor, Healer, Redeemer, Father, the Holy One, and the Most High to name a few. Oh the power in His name. Jesus, Jesus, Jesus.

Heavenly Father,

There is great power in your name. Help us to want to learn your names. Please give us the knowledge of the meanings of them to allow us to know you and love you even more.

In Jesus Name,

Amen

Matthew 22:37

Jesus replied, "'you must love the Lord your God with all your heart, all your soul, and all your mind.

41

WE ARE TOLD TO LOVE everyone and to have compassion for all. This is true, but there is a difference between helping the lost and someone in need and simply running with the wrong crowd.

If you know your character is being compromised by what you do or how you act it may be time to look in the mirror, ask yourself some hard questions, and make different choices and who you choose to spend time with.

Heavenly Father,

Thank you, Lord, for your truths. It is so easy to get caught up in the world. Help us to look to you for the characteristics we should aspire to and those we should be looking for in our friends. We pray you will place these right people in our lives to help correct our way. People that will help build and encourage the Christ like characters in us. Those that you so desire for us.

In Jesus Name,

Amen

1 Corinthians 15:33

Do not be misled: "Bad company corrupts good character."

42

WE HAVE SO MANY OPPORTUNITIES to give. This
can be with money, gifts, or even with our time, by serving others.
The decision of whom and where to give must be made between
you and God. It should not be done out of obligation or guilt, but
rather cheerfully, prayerfully, and generously.

Heavenly Father,

Help us to have a giving spirit and generous
heart. May you lead and guide us in whom and
how much we should give.

Bless the recipients as you have blessed us to be
able to share with them. Help us to appreciate all
you have given to us and to cheerfully give to
others.

In Jesus Name,

Amen

2 Corinthians 9:7

Each of you should give what you have decided in your heart
to give, not reluctantly or under compulsion, for God loves a
cheerful giver.

43

DO YOU EVER FEEL like you can't make anyone happy? Do you make decisions based on others' opinions, so they won't be angry? We should always try to live in peace with others, but we need to do so by obeying and pleasing God first and foremost. Not man.

Heavenly Father,

Please, Lord, help us to serve you first. To act and do what you would have us do. Pleasing you will always be the right decision. Allow us to experience true joy and happiness in our relationships, because we are obeying you.

Guard our hearts and minds.

In Jesus Name,

Amen

Galatians 1:10

Am I now trying to win the approval of human beings, or of God? Or am I trying to please people? If I were still trying to please people, I would not be a servant of Christ.

44

JESUS. He was blameless and without Sin as he walked this earth. However, He suffered temptations like we do. He cried out. We face not a single situation he did not face. Yet, He remained obedient. He relied on God, and Trusted Him. We can learn by His example.

Heavenly Father,

Bless us, Lord. Help us to trust and refrain from the sin that tempts us. Allow us to consider how Jesus reacted and refrained. Help us to do the same.

In Jesus Name,

Amen

Hebrews 5:8-10

While he lived on earth, anticipating death, Jesus cried out in pain and wept in sorrow as he offered up priestly prayers to God. Because he honored God, God answered him. Though he was God's Son, he learned trusting-obedience by what he suffered, just as we do.

Hebrews 5:8 New Living Translation

Even though Jesus was God's Son, he learned obedience from the things he suffered.

45

WHY IS IT SO HARD for us to listen to God and do right, even if we know he will heal us? We can hold tight to His promise that we will not have to suffer if we obey.

Heavenly Father,

Lord God, your promises are so clear and are completely full of hope!   Guide us daily to stop and consider the consequences to our decisions. We love you, Lord.   Thank you for the healing you promise.

In Jesus Name,

Amen

Exodus 15:26

He said, "If you will listen carefully to the voice of the Lord your God and do what is right in his sight, obeying his commands and keeping all his decrees, then I will not make you suffer any of the diseases I sent on the Egyptians; for I am the Lord who heals you.

46

DO YOU GROW WEARY from daily demands? Do you long for rest for your body and soul? Jesus promises the ultimate rest. Call on Him. Come near to Him. He will provide peace beyond our imagination.

Heavenly Father,

Lord God, we come to you with heavy burdens. These include health, financial, or relationship issues. For others it is work, haunting pasts, the fear of the future, or a recent loss of a loved one. Take these burdens, Lord. Heal us, strengthen us, and renew our hope! We thank you for carrying it all for us, and paying the ultimate price for us on the cross.

In Jesus Name,

Amen

Matthew 11:28

Then Jesus said, "Come to me, all of you who are weary and carry heavy burdens, and I will give you rest.

47

PRAYER IS SO POWERFUL. We are instructed to do it continually, without ceasing. To cry out, pouring all of our burdens unto Him.

We are to seek Him with Thanksgiving and to ask Him for the desires of our heart. We therefore should not be timid in prayer, but rather be confident and bold in our requests. We should pray with expectation that our prayers will be heard and undoubtedly answered.

Heavenly Father,

Lord, so very often we do not know which way to turn, or, we hold a prayer list longer than we care to admit, but that is never an issue for you. As we bring these things to you, help us to do so boldly. Allow us to pray with the full expectation and confidence that you will have the direction, solution, and perfectly timed answer.

In Jesus Name,

Amen

James 1:6

But when you ask, you must believe and not doubt, because the one who doubts is like a wave of the sea, blown and tossed by the wind.

48

TESTING, one – two – three - four... this is only a test...

Some days feel like a continuous test of our patience and grace.

Sometimes, we bite our tongues, walk away, or react gracefully.

Other times....well not so much. We may say more than we should, think the worst, or lash out with less than friendly reactions. Instead of blaming, fretting, asking why? We should ask, "Lord, what is it you want us to learn?" "What are you refining in me?"

Heavenly Father,

Thank you, Lord, for the reminder that every situation has a purpose. That regardless of good times, bad times, happy times, or painful ones, you, Lord, have the plan for our lives. You continue to define, refine and grow in us, so we might be like you. You continually grow our character through our situations and sufferings.

In Jesus Name,

Amen

Isaiah 48:10

I have refined you, but not as silver is refined. Rather, I have refined you in the furnace of suffering.

49

GIFTS... they come in all shapes and sizes. They are sometimes expected, yet other times quite the surprise. They are at times very expensive. However, our greatest gift is free. It is given cheerfully. We only need to choose to receive this special gift. Yes, our greatest gift is Jesus. He was blameless, born a man to walk this earth and die for our sins. He is the most precious gift we can choose to accept.

Heavenly Father,

Thank you, Lord, for coming to earth. For being born in the flesh. You made the ultimate sacrifice of leaving the glorious heaven and coming to earth to save us. We are grateful for you, Lord.

In Jesus Name,

Amen

Isaiah 9:6

For a child is born to us, a son is given to us. The government will rest on his shoulders. And he will be called: Wonderful Counselor, Mighty God, Everlasting Father, and Prince of Peace.

HERE ARE THE LYRICS of the lovely Song played at Christmas time. It is, of course written about Mary. Her wonder of why she was chosen to carry Jesus. That she sometimes has to wait for answers, and her realization that she needs God to hold her strong. That God in all His Holiness has the plan. We are like Mary in that we too need to depend on our Lord to hold us strong each and every day.

Lyrics of: *Breath of Heaven* -
(Written by Amy Grant & Chris Eaton)

I have travelled much moonless night
Cold and weary with a babe inside
And I wonder what I've done
Holy Father, you have come
And chosen me now to carry your son

I am waiting in a silent prayer
I am frightened by the load I bear
In a world as cold as stone
Must I walk this path alone?
Be with me now
Be with me now

Breath of heaven
Hold me together
Be forever near me
Breath of heaven Breath of heaven
Light up my darkness
Pour over me your holiness
For you are holy
Breath of heaven

Do you wonder as you watch my face
If a wiser one should have had my place

But I offer all I am for the mercy of your plan
Help me be strong
Help me be
Help me

Breath of heaven
Hold me together
Be forever near me
Breath of heaven
Breath of heaven
Lighten my darkness
Pour over me your holiness
For you are holy...

Heavenly Father,

Lord, help us to cling to you for our security. Help us, hold us, and be with us.

In Jesus Name,

Amen

Psalm 63:8

I cling to you; your strong right hand holds me securely.

51

WE ARE CALLED for a purpose. We are called to grow in faith and be Christ-like. We are called to obedience. This doesn't just happen. It takes preparation, planning, and deliberate focus. It then takes action, self-control, and the full acceptance of His grace in our lives.

Heavenly Father,

Help us, Lord to be alert, have a clear vision, and to be ready to act in accordance to your will. Allow us to accept your love freely. Lord, may this give us the desire to live out your purpose and live for you each and every day.   Doing so proudly, confidently, and always for your Glory.

In Jesus Name,

Amen

1 Peter 1:13

Therefore, preparing your minds for action, and being sober-minded, set your hope fully on the grace that will be brought to you at the revelation of Jesus Christ.

52

AS WE REFLECT ON THE PAST, we remember good, bad, busy, joy filled, stressful, fun filled, happy, and sad times. For some, time moved quickly, and for others, it did not.

We were never promised an easy life, but at times we wonder why it has to be so hard. As we look back we should do so with a grateful heart, always looking for the blessings in the midst of the chaos. We should recognize the rainbow after the rain, the bright side, and the amazing people who shared in this journey with us.

Heavenly Father,

Thank you, Lord, for all of the blessings you provided thus far. Thank you for the good times and bad. The ones filled with laughter, and for the growth that came from the trials. We love you, Lord. We find contentment in you through your love and grace.

In Jesus Name,

Amen

James 1:2-4

Dear brothers and sisters, when troubles of any kind come your way, consider it an opportunity for great joy. For you know that when your faith is tested, your endurance has a chance to grow. So let it grow, for when your endurance is fully developed, you will be perfect and complete, needing nothing.

Ephesians 5:20

Always giving thanks to God the Father for everything, in the name of our Lord Jesus Christ.

53

WHILE REFLECTING IS IMPORTANT, God wants us to look forward with expectation.

He has brand new things for us.

He already has it planned.

He actually has already started the work, if we look closely enough to see it. We can be assured of this. We just need to stay alert, pay attention, and watch in awe, focusing on Jesus.

Heavenly Father,

Lord, Thank you for all you have done, and we praise you for our futures. Help us to rely on you first, to be expecting you to lead the ways, and for the reassurance that you have control.

In Jesus Name,

Amen

Isaiah 43:16-19

I am the Lord, who opened a way through the waters, making a path right through the sea. I called forth the mighty army of Egypt with all its chariots and horses, to lay beneath the waves, dead, their lives snuffed out like candlewicks. But forget all that—it is nothing compared to what I'm going to do! For I'm going to do a brand-new thing. See, I have already begun! Don't you see it? I will make a road through the wilderness of the world for my people to go home, and create rivers for them in the desert.

54

SO OFTEN WE FEEL INADEQUATE because we haven't accomplished all of the things on the "to do" lists. We feel we have failed because our long-term goals seem out of reach.

The truth is, we are not asked to be perfect. We are just asked to continue onward and to not give up. To do this, we have to focus on the goal, not look back, not let obstacles detour us.

Heavenly Father,

Help us, Lord, as we continue to work at our goals, and to not be discouraged by setbacks. Allow us the freedom from focusing on the past. Rather, help us to keep focusing on the goal one day at a time. I pray our goals, first and foremost, are to trust you, to rely on your will for us and your hope for our futures. Thank you, Lord, for all you have done and all you have planned for us.

In Jesus Name,

Amen

Philippians 3:13

No, dear brothers and sisters, I have not achieved it, but I focus on this one thing: Forgetting the past and looking forward to what lies ahead.

55

HAVE YOU EVER GOTTEN A SPECIAL MESSAGE
out of the blue from a friend, at just the right time? Have you had
a friend on your heart and mind and you reach out, only to hear
they have been struggling with or have been excited about recent
happenings in their lives. This is not an accident, but rather a
relationship orchestrated by our Creator. God intends for us to
have many acquaintances, but a few true friends. They know us
authentically.

Heavenly Father,

Thank you, Lord, for the true friends you give us.
They are the ones that get us, and that
understand our struggles, pains, and desires.
Help us to recognize these friendships and
continue to nurture them. Most of all, Lord, we
thank you for the friend we have in you.

In Jesus Name,

Amen

Proverbs 18:24

Friends come and friends go, but a true friend sticks by you
like family.

56

WE ARE ALL TEMPTED by sin. It comes in many forms, and frankly seems to be "the way it is" in today's world. Not taking part in it feels like rejection, or a lack of acceptance. We need to be obedient in the truth, do what is right, and ask God to help us to rule over the sin, regardless of what the world says. If we do, we will find freedom and abundant Joy.

Heavenly Father,

Help us, Lord, to obey, do right, and not conform to the sins of the world. We know if we do we will be healed, find true freedom, and experience abundantly more than we could desire in our lives. Thank you, Lord, for wanting this for us.

In Jesus Name,

Amen

Genesis 4:7

If you do what is right, will you not be accepted? But if you do not do what is right, sin is crouching at your door; it desires to have you, but you must rule over it."

57

WE ALL HAVE TASKS that we have to do. Some seem easy or routine, while others seem overwhelming or unattainable. Some feel like they have an eternal purpose, while others feel meaningless. Regardless, God promises if we commit everything to Him, and trust Him, he will help us.

Heavenly Father,

Thank you, Lord, for the compassion you have for us. It is hard to understand how you can care about all of the small details of the tasks we have to do, but we are grateful that you do. We know by experience if we pray about the task, no matter the size, you answer. You provide the way, the peace, and the vision of the outcome through it all.

In Jesus Name,

Amen

Psalm 37:5

Commit everything you do to the Lord. Trust him, and he will help you.

58

ALTHOUGH WE GET SO BUSY and don't think of God's presence every moment, He is always with us. This is so reassuring in the good and the bad times. The important thing is to be confident of his presence. To acknowledge his goodness in the good and to trust him to hold us steady in the difficult times.

Heavenly Father,

Thank you for always being with us. Help us, Lord, to be mindful of your presence. We are grateful for your faithfulness to never leave or forsake us.

In Jesus Name,

Amen

Psalm 16:8

I know the Lord is always with me. I will not be shaken, for he is right beside me.

59

EVERYTHING HAS ITS SEASON. The seasons of the year, winter, spring, summer, and fall. The seasons of growth: infancy to maturity, seed to sprout, or from famine to feast. The seasons in our earthly relationships can go from close to distant. Regardless of the season, Remember God is in control and we just need to Trust Him and His timing. He will carry us through, no matter what.

Heavenly Father,

Lord, Thank you for the reminder that everything has its time, place and purpose. Everything is placed intentionally in its season for the good of those who love you.

In Jesus Name,

Amen

Ecclesiastes 3:1

For everything there is a season, a time for every activity under heaven.

60

THE SABBATH, the 7th day, Sunday, the Lord's Day... no matter what you call it, should be a day of rest and free of work. It doesn't mean you must sleep all day. Rather it means to spend the day worshipping God, giving thanks for all He has done, doing things you enjoy, and refueling for the week ahead.

Heavenly Father,

Thank you, Lord, for being the example of working and resting. Thanks for the restoration this day provides. We worship and praise you, Lord.

In Jesus Name,

Amen

Genesis 2:2

On the seventh day God had finished his work of creation, so he rested from all his work.

61

LISTENING... we often think we are better at it then we probably are. Our human nature causes us to start considering the conclusion, resolution, and sometimes even the expected emotion... all of that when we should be listening. Jesus showed the perfect example for listening. He listened, waited, and remained patient. He often would ask a question for clarification. We can learn so much by His example. By following this example we can truly learn to understand what others are saying and see their perspective more clearly.

Heavenly Father,

Thank you for the example of listening by Jesus. We are grateful that you truly listen to us and don't quickly get angry at us! Help us to be like that with others.

In Jesus Name,

Amen

James 1:19

My dear brothers and sisters, take note of this: Everyone should be quick to listen, slow to speak and slow to become angry.

DURING AND RIGHT AFTER weekly Sermons, we have a heightened appreciation for our Pastors, Worship Leaders, and Staff at our Churches. We then leave and get busy, and while we appreciate them, we may not remember them in our prayers throughout the week.

However, as instructed we should honor and pray for them regularly. They work tirelessly to share the good news of Jesus Christ and instruct us in the right way to live.

Heavenly Father,

Thank you each and every day for our Church Elders, Pastors, Worship, Discipleship, and various other Leaders and Staff in our Churches. We pray for them for strength as they serve. We also pray for their spouses and families for their sacrifice. Bless these Leaders, as they continue to bring more and more people to believe and follow you.

In Jesus Name,

Amen

1 Thessalonians 5:12

Dear brothers, honor the officers of your church who work hard among you and warn you against all that is wrong.

WE HAVE ALL SAID AND HEARD THINGS LIKE: "nothing like hitting us when we are down", "that was salt in the wounds", "it's one thing after another", or "we can't catch a break". When we are at our weakest the attacks feel the strongest. But in our weakness, Jesus is strong, loves us, and carries us. This reminds me of the familiar song we learned as Children.... :)

Jesus loves me this I know
For the Bible tells me so
Little ones to him belong
They are weak but he is strong

Heavenly Father,

Thank you, Lord, for your strength in our times when we are overwhelmed, tired, worn or simply under attack. You are our one and only hope and support. Thank you for being with us always.

In Jesus Name,

Amen

Psalm 18:18

They attacked me at a moment when I was in distress, but the Lord supported me.

64

THERE ARE CAUSES worth fighting for.

However, to fight for the sake of fighting is foolish. In all of our interactions, we should stop before speaking, be respectful, and mindful of our language both verbal and body. This will promote honor and reduce foolish confrontations.

Heavenly Father,

Guard our hearts, minds, and mouths. Allow our interactions to glorify you and not deem us foolish. Help us to see ourselves as others see us.

In Jesus Name,

Amen

Proverbs 20:3

Avoiding a fight is a mark of honor; only fools insist on quarreling.

WHEN YOU ARE in the heat of the moment, the thick of things, or at a point when any decision made will have lasting impact, know that there is a source that you should consult with first. He is there to listen, and is the only that is on your side 100 % of the time. Yes, that One and only is Jesus. He can provide peace in the chaos, wisdom and discernment in His Word. Give Him your cares, decisions, and troubles.

Heavenly Father,

Thank you for the reassurance that you are the One and only constant. Because of you, we do not have to fear. You provide wisdom in the toughest of situations, and will always be there to fight the battles for us.

In Jesus Name,

Amen

Psalm 118:5-6

When hard pressed, I cried to the Lord; he brought me into a spacious place. The Lord is with me; I will not be afraid. What can mere mortals do to me?

CORRECTION, DISCIPLINE, AND TRUTH... we all need it and should be hearing it. The difference is our reaction and subsequent action we take to redirect. If we hear it and dismiss it without consideration, then we gain nothing. We are also setting ourselves up to lose. However, if we take it to heart and make the necessary changes we gain understanding and growth.

Heavenly Father,

Discipline and correction is hard to hear at times, but we know it is a necessary part of growth. I pray we are open to this at any time. That we accept it, learn from it, and grow in the understanding it brings. May the fruits that are produced by the pruning glorify You.

In Jesus Name,

Amen

Proverbs 15:32

If you reject discipline, you only harm yourself; but if you listen to correction, you grow in understanding.

IF YOU ARE A LEADER of an organization or a leader in your family, do your best, be bold and diligent, and God will be with you. He will guide you and keep you regardless of the circumstances and situations.

Heavenly Father,

Thank you, Lord, for your promise to help us and to guide us as long as we remain faithful and steadfast in our responsibilities.

In Jesus Name,

Amen

2 Chronicles 19:11

"Amariah the chief priest is in charge of all cases regarding the worship of God; Zebadiah son of Ishmael, the leader of the tribe of Judah, is in charge of all civil cases; the Levites will keep order in the courts. Be bold and diligent. And God be with you as you do your best."

68

JESUS WAS THE ULTIMATE EXAMPLE of paying it forward.

When you accept him, your sins are covered!

Yes, ALL sins, past, present, and future. We need to confess and turn from them. We do this by coming back to God, not hiding in the sin, but seeking what has already been paid for.

Heavenly Father,

We thank you for the cross. We thank you for the eternal life you promise us through the forgiveness of our sins, the belief and hope we have in you. I pray we all accept this, and even if we slip away in our daily sins, we will earnestly come back to you.

In Jesus Name,

Amen

2 Corinthians 5:19-20

For God was in Christ, reconciling the world to himself, no longer counting people's sins against them. And he gave us this wonderful message of reconciliation. So we are Christ's ambassadors; God is making his appeal through us. We speak for Christ when we plead, "Come back to God!"

69

THIS IS THE DAY AND AGE of HGTV, DIY, Pinterest, and all of the transformation before-and-after shows. It seems like we are always looking to refresh, renew, and restore. We do so to our homes, our landscapes, and our exterior look and appearances. These resources are fantastic, but let's not forget the BEST interior decorator we have is the Holy Spirit. God sent Him to work in us, and to continually refresh and renew us.

Heavenly Father,

Thank you, Lord, for caring so much about our internal and external design. Thank you for the step by step instructions you provide in your Word. To your Glory, God, for the positive change and upgrades you make in us, all for the eternal purpose.

In Jesus Name,

Amen

Psalm 23:3

He refreshes my soul. He guides me along the right paths for his name's sake.

DO YOU EVER FEEL LIKE your life is a mystery, an unfinished puzzle, or partially written story?

At times, our walk is simply unclear and we struggle to see ourselves as we were created. But, we do not need to fear, God knows it. He knows us. Until we can see and know all, when we are face to face with Him in eternity, we will see what He needs us to see. For the rest, we must Trust in Him, seek Him for clarity and be confident that we are His, and He will hold us through the unknowns.

Heavenly Father,

Thank you, Lord, for holding the plan and revealing what we need as we go. We look forward to the clarity you will one day provide. We thank you for preparing us daily. Thank you for creating us uniquely for your purpose.

In Jesus Name,

Amen

1 Corinthians 13:12

We don't yet see things clearly. We're squinting in a fog, peering through a mist. But it won't be long before the weather clears and the sun shines bright! We'll see it all then, see it all as clearly as God sees us, knowing him directly just as he knows us!

71

THE ENEMY WORKS HARD to place self-doubt in our minds, but don't believe it. Rather, believe that God has great things for you. It is easy to tell others that God Loves them, and has Chosen them. It is much harder to say this about yourself. Say it, practice it. Pray about believing it. This knowledge and acceptance will change your life!

Heavenly Father,

Thank you, Lord, for loving me and choosing me. I pray everyone reading this will personalize this promise to them self. Our eternity is a free gift by accepting you, but our individual relationship with you is important for how we live out our lives on earth. The closer we are to you and the more we know about you the more we recognize how you are working in our lives. We then want to share this with others, so they too can experience the joy that you bring; to your glory, Lord!

In Jesus Name,

Amen

1 Peter 2:9

But you are not like that, for you are a chosen people. You are royal priests, a holy nation, and God's very own possession. As a result, you can show others the goodness of God, for he called you out of the darkness into his wonderful light.

DOES WORRY EVER keep you up, and then what you were worried about never happens? Do you fret over something that won't be resolved for some time in the future? Yet, we stew on it now, even though it is out of our hands. The Word says we are not to worry tomorrow.

Heavenly Father,

Thank you, Lord, for guarding our hearts and minds from unreasonable and unnecessary worry. Help us to trust you and live in the spirit of praise and thanksgiving without worrying about tomorrow.

In Jesus Name,

Amen

Matthew 6:34

"So don't worry about tomorrow, for tomorrow will bring its own worries. Today's trouble is enough for today.

DO YOU EVER FEEL LIKE you are down in the dumps, down on your luck, or down to feeling nothing?

Does the situation appear to have no way to improve?

Is it causing pain and suffering?

Do you feel a lack of peace and contentment?

Take heart. Jesus overcame the world. Although He didn't promise a life without trials and sorrows, He did bear it all for us. He is bigger than all of the sadness and pain. He will provide us peace and joy in the midst of it all. Trust Him.

Heavenly Father,

Thank you, Lord, for the reminder that you are our source for peace. Your promises are the hope we hold on to in our times of doubt. Lord, we thank you, for bearing it all on the cross and overcoming on our behalf.

In Jesus Name,

Amen

John 16:33

I have told you all this so that you may have peace in me. Here on earth you will have many trials and sorrows. But take heart, because I have overcome the world."

74

MANY WONDER how this book is written. Where do the words come from? It is simple; they are inspired by God's Word. His truths, placed on the heart of an ordinary person to encourage others to press on, to steady our steps, and to put our full faith in the One and only Savior of the world. JESUS.

Heavenly Father,

Thank you for using me and this forum to reach others for your Glory! Please continue to bless us with the right word at the right time. That will revive and pick us up when we are falling away. The Word and truths encourage and support us when we are weak and have weary knees.

In Jesus Name,

Amen

Job 4:4

Your words have supported those who were falling; you encouraged those with shaky knees.

75

IT TAKES A SEED PLANTED to produce a crop. These seeds need to be nurtured with the right amount of water. Not too little to leave them dry and parched. Not too much to drown them out. Sometimes they will grow quickly in a season, and sometimes it takes years. Regardless, with proper soil, patience, perseverance, and perfect timing, the results can be amazing.

Heavenly Father,

We thank you for the results of seeds of your love and truth planted; sometimes years ago, now showing growth. Thank you for your compassion, grace and patience during the nurturing process. May it be all for your Glory!

In Jesus Name,

Amen

Luke 8:15

But the seed on good soil stands for those with a noble and good heart, who hear the word, retain it, and by persevering produce a crop.

76

THERE ARE THINGS YOU ARE TOLD that are meant to be kept secret and confidential. Other things are meant to be shared and passed on.

The Good News of Jesus is absolutely one to be shared with many. The best way to do this is by telling others how God has worked in and changed your life. How His grace has covered you, how His promises have been revealed to you, and that His hope is carrying you through.

Heavenly Father,

Lord, Thank you, for all that you have done. Allow us the opportunity to share your Good News with others. You have promised that each experience we have had has been for a purpose. Each has created our story, which is always a part of your story. Thank you for your truth and grace.

In Jesus Name,

Amen

Colossians 1:6

This same Good News that came to you is going out all over the world. It is bearing fruit everywhere by changing lives, just as it changed your lives from the day you first heard and understood the truth about God's wonderful grace.

IN TODAY'S WORLD OF TECHNOLOGY, if our devices freeze, run slow or throw an error message, we naturally hit restart. This gives them a chance to regroup and fix themselves. Most of the time this is all that is needed to get them to start where we left off - not having to start from scratch or reloading all the data.

In our spiritual walk, we often need to hit our restart buttons, remembering it is a chance to fix things. We have the knowledge; it is stored in our hearts and mind. We know better, we just need to surrender.

Rather than continuing in the cycle, we need to reset, repent, and go deeper in our relationship with Jesus, further understanding and growing in faith and letting go of the things that trip us up and slow us down.

Heavenly Father,

Thank you, Lord, for the reminder that as we repent, we need to redirect and restart. Then to take what we know and continue to grow and mature like you want us to.

In Jesus Name,

Amen

Hebrews 6:1

So let us stop going over the basic teachings about Christ again and again. Let us go on instead and become mature in our understanding. Surely we don't need to start again with the fundamental importance of repenting from evil deeds and placing our faith in God.

78

FEAR CAN OVERTAKE US when we consider the "what ifs", the "unknown outcomes", and "uncharted territories". But if we say no to the fears and yes to trusting Him, we are promised rest. Trust Him. Pray. Give Him the fear. Rest in Him.

Heavenly Father,

Lord, take our fears and provide the rest that will help us sleep soundly. Help us to trust you. Settle the churning in our souls and free us from the evil one who puts this fear in our minds. We trust you, Lord, and know you are always fighting on our behalf.

In Jesus Name,

Amen

Proverbs 3:24

You can go to bed without fear; you will lie down and sleep soundly.

HAVE YOU EVER uttered a simple prayer to ask for someone to change, then afterwards nothing changes and we are back into the same old routine?

This could happen because we may need to ask God to change and improve us, not others. We may also need to examine our motives for the change. To be sure they are in line with God's will and plan. If they are, we can be assured God will work to accomplish far more than we could have ever asked in their lives, but if it is not, we may be the ones he is molding.

Heavenly Father,

Thank you, Lord, for your mighty power that works in us when we are willing to change. You provide so much more than we can ever imagine when we Trust you and let you drive. We love you, Lord. To all the Glory be unto you.

In Jesus Name,

Amen

Ephesians 3:20

Now all glory to God, who is able, through his mighty power at work within us, to accomplish infinitely more than we might ask or think.

DO YOU EVER STRUGGLE with picking out the perfect outfit? Not wanting it to be too dressy or too casual, asking the questions, wondering if it will fit just right, if others will like it, or simply if it will make the wrong statement. In our daily spiritual walk we don't have to worry about the perfect outfit. We have access to the Full Armor of God. When clothed in it we can be confident in the mighty power God has intended for us.

Heavenly Father,

Thank you, Lord, for the perfect outfit for every occasion. We thank you that we can stand firm in our faith and resist the evil one when we rely on your power and strength of the armor.

In Jesus Name,

Amen

Ephesians 6:10-11

A final word: Be strong in the Lord and in his mighty power. Put on all of God's armor so that you will be able to stand firm against all strategies of the devil.

SOMETIMES, THE TASKS BEFORE US may seem out of reach, even if we have followed each and every step along the way. We get so close, down to the 11th hour. The closer we get, the further the outcome feels, because we are tired and weary. Rather than give up, this is the time to surrender to God. To ask for His strength, because we can do anything, accomplish the impossible, and finish the race through the strength of Christ.

Heavenly Father,

Lord God when we face the impossible we know we can depend on you and your strength. Thank you for carrying us when we are weak, tired, and feeling hopeless. Help us to draw on this strength.

In Jesus Name,

Amen

Philippians 4:13

For I can do everything through Christ who gives me strength.

GOD USES THE ORDINARY to share the Good News. He uses the simple everyday interactions in our workplaces, schools, churches, and even while shopping to work through us. The interactions can vary from a smile, telling someone to have a good day, listening to another's struggle, or sharing experiences of how God has worked in our lives. These moments are orchestrated in advance, each with a purpose and a choice for us to be positive and uplifting.

Heavenly Father,

Thank you, Lord, for using us as vessels to share you with the world. Help us to continue to grow in the knowledge of your truths. I pray we are aware that our daily interactions can produce a sweet scent to others, if we remain positive.

In Jesus Name,

Amen

2 Corinthians 2:14

But thank God! He has made us his captives and continues to lead us along in Christ's triumphal procession. Now he uses us to spread the knowledge of Christ everywhere, like a sweet perfume.

83

DO YOU EVER FEEL DEPRESSED after watching the news or scanning your social media page? We live in a complex world of differing opinions, where hurting others with words or violence is often accepted as normal. Don't be discouraged. There is still good in the world. We just have to look past the darkness to the ultimate source of light. This is found in the Word of God. The teachings are made for even the ordinary to understand. When we let the light of His word be our guide, we see hope, deliverance, forgiveness, and peace.

Heavenly Father,

Thank you, Lord, for being our source of light. Help us to remember to seek your Word to learn your truth. Allow your light to shine in our daily lives, so we may also be a light to others.
Thank you for the grace, guidance, and goodness you provide.

In Jesus Name,

Amen

Psalm 119:130

Break open your words; let the light shine out, let ordinary people see the meaning.

84

DO WHAT IS RIGHT. Press on. Stay the course. Focus on the goal. All of these are statements we use to encourage ourselves, or others, to stay strong. However, despite the words, there are times we grow tired. Don't fear, God promises we will reap the harvest if we don't give up.

Heavenly Father,

Lord, thank you for your perfect timing, and the rest you provided to strengthen us in the wait. Your ways are so far better than our imagination. Help us not to give up and not to give in. Allow us to let you work in us and through us, for your Glory.

In Jesus Name,

Amen

Galatians 6:9

Let us not become weary in doing good, for at the proper time we will reap a harvest if we do not give up.

85

THERE ARE TIMES IN OUR LIVES when things go from bad to good in what seems like an instant, after we have prayed for relief, a change of heart, or even a miracle. Don't miss the fact that the praise for the change belongs to God alone. He is the miracle maker. He is the One that saves relationships, businesses, Churches, the sick, the lost, and those under spiritual attack.

Heavenly Father,

We praise you, Lord, for your work in our lives. You take the bad to good and the good to great right before our eyes. You care about the smallest of details in our lives. Thank you!

In Jesus Name,

Amen

Deuteronomy 10:21

He alone is your God, the only one who is worthy of your praise, the one who has done these mighty miracles that you have seen with your own eyes.

WE ARE SO BLESSED by the encouragement we receive from God's promises as we read his Word, listen to sermons, or uplifting worship music. We don't always get encouraged from others however, nor do we give encouragement like we should. In His word, God has challenged us to be more Christ-like. Let's take on that challenge one day at a time.

Heavenly Father,

Forgive us, Lord, for the times we are more judgmental than supportive to others. Help us to look for opportunities to see the good in people and to express our sincere appreciation to encourage and build them up each day.

In Jesus Name,

Amen

Romans 15:5

May the God who gives endurance and encouragement give you the same attitude of mind toward each other that Christ Jesus had.

THERE IS NO SPECIFIC TIME OR WAY TO PRAY.
It doesn't have to be on Sunday. Nor does it have to be formal,
elegant, or perfect. God is available 24/7 365, and longs to hear
from us. Just talk to Him like a friend. Tell him your struggles, the
things you are thankful for, and the people in your life that are in
need. He will hear your prayers and answer them.

Heavenly Father,

Thank you, Lord, for always being available and
hearing our cries of distress. You already know
everything Lord, yet you still want us to express
our feelings to you. Thank you for being our
friend.

In Jesus Name,

Amen

Psalm 55:17

Morning, noon, and night I cry out in my distress, and the Lord
hears my voice.

DOUBT IS SNEAKY. It can creep in when we least expect it. It often is disguised by busyness, a joking comment, or an unexplained look from a loved one. The evil one is the culprit behind the doubts. He uses our weaknesses to bind us. However, we have immediate access to being free from the evil one, released of the crippling feelings of doubt, and to receive renewed hope.

The moment doubt enters your mind, Pray!

Heavenly Father,

Lord, Thank you for the compassion you have for us, the freedom you provide, and the everlasting hope we can have just for believing you! Thank you, Lord, for your victory that was accomplished on the cross.

In Jesus Name,

Amen

Psalm 94:19

When doubts filled my mind, your comfort gave me renewed hope and cheer.

89

DO YOU EVER NEED a reminder to be nice, show kindness, or to remain loyal? It is not always easy in this world, but these qualities really are easy to give to others. They are free, don't require a lot of upfront work, and have eternal results. Just take a breath and think about how Jesus treated others.

Heavenly Father,

Thank you, Lord, for the loyalty and kindness you show us every day. You're so patient with us, even when we don't deserve it. We love you, Lord!

In Jesus Name,

Amen

Proverbs 3:3

Never let loyalty and kindness leave you! Tie them around your neck as a reminder. Write them deep within your heart.

CHRISTIAN FELLOWSHIP is a time to meet brothers and sisters in Christ for the purpose of encouraging, motivating, and learning from each other. These times are ultimately meant to help us grow in the knowledge of Jesus, and to share the Good News for the Glory of the Kingdom.

Heavenly Father,

Thank you, Lord, for the opportunities we have to meet with other Christians in small groups, large Church services, and in the one on one conversation. Bless these meetings with truth and love. Help us to continue to seek these times and not let distractions keep us away.

In Jesus Name,

Amen

Hebrews 10:24-25

Let us think of ways to motivate one another to acts of love and good works. And let us not neglect our meeting together, as some people do, but encourage one another, especially now that the day of his return is drawing near.

91

SACRIFICE MAY initially feel like losing something, being withheld a pleasure, or restricting ourselves. Yet, ultimately obedience to God relieves our pain and suffering and provides freedom. Jesus, although he did not sin, knew obedience, sacrifice, and suffering. Despite it all, he obeyed, and bore it all on the cross for our freedom.

Heavenly Father,

Forgive us, Lord, for being so selfish when you ask us to be obedient in a specific area of our lives. Rather than saying "Yes Lord ", we hold on, make excuses, and put off obeying. Help us to trust and understand that the freedom is in the sacrifice. Thank you for sacrificing it all for us.

In Jesus Name,

Amen

Hebrews 5:8

Even though Jesus was God's Son, he learned obedience from the things he suffered.

WITH THE BUSYNESS of the world today and all of the demands, we often "blink" and cannot believe how fast the years have gone by. We realize how important it is to love and appreciate our families as we age. We may feel sad because we wished we had spent more time, or smile, as we reflect on the memories. Regardless, we are instructed by God to encourage young women to love their husbands and children in the now, so they too do not miss anything as they "blink".

Heavenly Father,

Lord God we are so grateful for the relationships, marriages, and families you have given us. As older women, I pray, we use every opportunity to encourage the young women to love their husbands and children. Allow them to treasure the moments. Please bless them, Lord.

In Jesus Name,

Amen

Titus 2:4

So that they may encourage the young women to love their husbands, to love their children.

93

SOMETIMES WE JUST NEED a little hope, courage, and strength to get through the day. The Good News is that we don't have to look very far if we have trust and faith in God. We simply need to ask him, draw near to Him, and give our cares over to him. When we do this our strength, courage, and hope will be restored.

Heavenly Father,

We thank you, Lord, for restoration and the hope we can only get in you. Some days, we have to deal with situation or people that can be overwhelming and difficult, but the reassurance that you are always near and available is all we need Lord.

In Jesus Name,

Amen

Psalm 31:24

So be strong and courageous, all you who put your hope in the Lord!

GRACE AND COMPASSION are what our Lord wants for us. Yet, He is just and fair, so it is in His perfect timing that He will shower us with these blessing. Until then, we need to wait, trust, and continue to have faith.

Heavenly Father,

We wait on you, Lord, for your blessings of grace and compassion. Thank you, Lord for loving us so much. We are grateful for your justice, fairness, and blessings.

In Jesus Name,

Amen

Isaiah 30:18

Yet the Lord longs to be gracious to you; therefore he will rise up to show you compassion. For the Lord is a God of justice. Blessed are all who wait for him.

95

HAVE YOU EVER tried to get ahead of God?

Meaning you trusted Him, but before He had a chance to bring the situation to completion in His way you took matters into your own hands. You made choices to do it your way, instead of waiting on God. You may have gotten results that seemed good, but God's results would have been great. They would have provided a witness to others of His faithfulness, given you freedom from the stronghold of that area, and likely been an abundantly better outcome than expected.

Waiting is worth it.

Heavenly Father,

Forgive us, Lord, for trying to be in control. Allow us to understand that you have better timing, better methods of handling things, and better results. We love you, Lord.

In Jesus Name,

Amen

Numbers 20:12

But the Lord said to Moses and Aaron, "Because you did not trust me enough to demonstrate my holiness to the people of Israel, you will not lead them into the land I am giving them!"

TRUTH... it is at times hard to give and hard to receive. Why? Because it hurts, and it can so easily offend or be misunderstood. Actually, according to scriptures, the truth can set you free! Holding back truth in a relationship can cause trust issues - and not being aware of truth can prevent healing. There really is freedom in truth!

Heavenly Father,

Help us to not be afraid of telling or hearing the truth. Help us to be humble and open to it, Lord, allowing healing and freedom as we release truth in our lives. We thank you for the truth in your Word. We know it is always the one true validation to truth!

In Jesus Name,

Amen

John 8:32

Then you will know the truth, and the truth will set you free.

97

THE LOVE THE LORD OUR GOD has for us is beyond our sight, our imagination, or our logical thinking. It is unfailing, incomprehensible, and unwavering. Yet, we feel it in our hearts, our souls, and our minds. It comforts us, strengthens us, and carries us through.

Heavenly Father,

Thank you, Lord for your faithfulness and your love. It is far reaching but ever present in us. Help us to be aware of your presence. We are grateful for you, Lord!

In Jesus Name,

Amen

Psalm 36:5

Your unfailing love, O Lord, is as vast as the heavens; your faithfulness reaches beyond the clouds.

WE ALL KNOW what worry feels like. We don't like it for ourselves, our family, or our friends. We know that encouraging words from others helps to take our minds off the worry for a bit, and helps to cheer us up. Let's remember this as we see and hear of others who are suffering with worry. Be compassionate to them and offer them an encouraging word, it can make a big difference in not only their day, but yours as well.

Heavenly Father,

Thank you, Lord, for the reminder that others need encouragement as much as we do, especially as the worries of life weigh heavily on them. Allow us to show them the compassion and care that you modeled for us.

In Jesus Name,

Amen

Proverbs 12:25

Worry weighs a person down; an encouraging word cheers a person up.

99

GIVING THANKS TO THE LORD is something we cannot do enough of. The work of God never ceases. He never tires. We see His blessings in our relationships, our work, and even our hobbies. He cares about it all. We can never out do Him. He knows our heart's desires. He deserves all honor and praise repeatedly and often.

Heavenly Father,

Thank You. Thank You. Thank you, Lord, for all you have done in our lives. We praise you for the work you do in us daily. We pray that all of the Glory comes back to you, Lord. You are so worthy of all of the praise.

In Jesus Name,

Amen

Psalm 109:30

But I will give repeated thanks to the Lord, praising him to everyone.

100

IT IS A PRIVILEGE AND JOY to lift others up, and to share God's Good News. This is solely done by His mighty power, grace, and the Holy Spirit working in and through us. It is a win-win for everyone, no matter if you are the giver or the receiver. We are blessed and God is always Glorified.

Heavenly Father,

We thank you, Lord, for the privilege to serve you, spreading your Good News filled with great love, power, and grace. We thank you for your faithfulness and patience with us as we continue to reach out to others. It can be out of our comfort zone, but when it is for you and your purpose we can Trust in you for the strength to continue.

In Jesus Name,

Amen

Ephesians 3:7

By God's grace and mighty power, I have been given the privilege of serving him by spreading this Good News.

101

BEING DISCOURAGED AND SAD can creep in without notice. Sometimes these feelings occur when things seem to be going very well. We wonder, "Why do we feel this way". This is normal, yes normal! We can stew, or we can ask God to reveal the reason, we can simply seek comfort. We are so fortunate that God is always ready for us to put our hope in Him again and again, to praise Him for the good and look to him to relieve the sadness.

Heavenly Father,

Thank you, Lord, for the reassurance that you are always there for us. Always ready for us to rely on your strength and not ours, in good times and sad times. We love you, Lord.

In Jesus Name,

Amen

Psalm 42:11

Why am I discouraged? Why is my heart so sad? I will put my hope in God! I will praise him again—my Savior and my God!

102

IN A WORLD THAT IS EASILY SHAKEN, we don't have to be. When we place our faith in Him, and receive the Kingdom, we are given the peace that passes all understanding. Oh we are grateful, thankful, and worship Him in reverence and awe.

Heavenly Father,

Thank you, Lord, for the stability you provide us through the peace we have in you. You are Holy and worthy of all of our praise. Thank you, Lord, for all you do and all you are.

In Jesus Name,

Amen

Hebrews 12:28

Since we are receiving a Kingdom that is unshakable, let us be thankful and please God by worshiping him with holy fear and awe.

HAVE YOU EVER BEEN through a spiritual drought? During this time you may have felt far from grace, slightly unworthy, and frankly like God was not working in your life.

This cannot be further from the truth. During the silent times and the dry seasons, God is working harder than ever on our desires. Trust in Him, Believe His Faithfulness, and Receive the Power He provides.

Heavenly Father,

Lord, thank you for always working in us. I pray we can recognize what you are doing. Thank you and praise you regardless of the season.

In Jesus Name,

Amen

Philippians 2:13

For God is working in you, giving you the desire and the power to do what pleases him.

104

WISDOM IS SOMETHING WE NEED in making all of our decisions and choices. We seek it out by using Google, asking our friends their thoughts, and sometimes even asking total strangers. The answers can be very confusing at times. For clarity, we should first seek God, ask Him for wisdom, and compare our decisions to what His Word says.

Heavenly Father,

Thank you, Lord, for your truths. We trust you first for our wisdom. Help us to not depend on our own searches or understanding, but depend on your word to shine light on our choices.

In Jesus Name,

Amen

James 1:5

If you need wisdom, ask our generous God, and he will give it to you. He will not rebuke you for asking.

105

REMEMBER, do not forget, and hold on to the memories. For some, this is not possible, but for most of us we are told to do so. It is easy to go on without remembering where we came from, the experiences we have had, and all of the blessings we've received along the way.

Heavenly Father,

Thank you, Lord, for the reminder to remember. We are in awe, Lord, when we look back and remember all you have done. The path that you have provided is perfect.

In Jesus Name,

Amen

Deuteronomy 4:9

"But watch out! Be careful never to forget what you yourself have seen. Do not let these memories escape from your mind as long as you live! And be sure to pass them on to your children and grandchildren.

106

IN THIS LIFE, keeping score is often used and needed. Keeping score is used in sporting events to determine the winners and losers, and often, the overall champion. In school it tells if a student passes or fails, and shows how they rank against other their peers. Other times, though, score keeping can actually be hurtful, can cause hard feelings, be perceived improperly, and can simply not be appropriate.

Heavenly Father,

Help us, Lord, to be sure competition and score keeping are done appropriately. Guide our hearts and minds to not keep track of others faults, but rather allow us to work on ourselves and our own shortcomings.

In Jesus Name,

Amen

John 4:1-2

Now Jesus learned that the Pharisees had heard that he was gaining and baptizing more disciples than John—although in fact it was not Jesus who baptized, but his disciples.

WE ARE TO live like Jesus. We are to live out our purpose and plan. How is this? How do we accomplish this? We do it by showing grace, kindness and compassion, providing mercy, loving others unconditionally, and being forgiving. Basically, it is treating others with the respect we desire from others. We are to listen, not judge, and remember that others are likely going through more than we know.

Heavenly Father,

Lord God, Help us to serve as you serve, to love like you love, and have the generous spirit that you have towards us. Guide us through this, as it is not of the world, but rather of you.

In Jesus Name,

Amen

Matthew 5:48

"In a word, what I'm saying is, grow up. You're kingdom subjects. Now live like it. Live out your God-created identity. Live generously and graciously toward others, the way God lives toward you."

About the Author

My name is Lisa Wirtner, a follower of Jesus, wife, mom, grandmother, and friend. I've always had a passion for encouraging others, to provide strength to those struggling, or sometimes an ear to those who need to talk. Driven by faith and compassion, I started a blog. I used this newfound outreach to share HIS hope, but more so to lift up my friends and family, providing them with encouragement as they dealt with hardship and doubt. Faced with a number of questions, I then decided to transition from a daily blog to the publishing world, hoping that my devotionals can touch more people, providing a positive uplift whenever needed. I hope you enjoy *Between us Ordinary Peeps,* my first book, and learn that strength can be found inside all of us. We just need to know where to look!

References

Holy Bible, New Living Translation. Copyright © 1996, 2004, 2015 – Tyndale House Publishers Inc., Carol Stream, IL. BibleGateway.com, online.

"Breath of Heaven", Lyrics - written by Chris Eaton, Amy Lee Grant. Copyright © BMG Rights Management US LLC. Google Play Music, online.

"Trust in You", Lyrics – written by Lauren Daigle, Michael Farren, Paul Mabury. Copyright © SONY/ATV Music Publishing LLC, Capitol Christian Music Group. Google Play Music, online.